W9-BJF-439

DINOWORLD
Stegosaurus

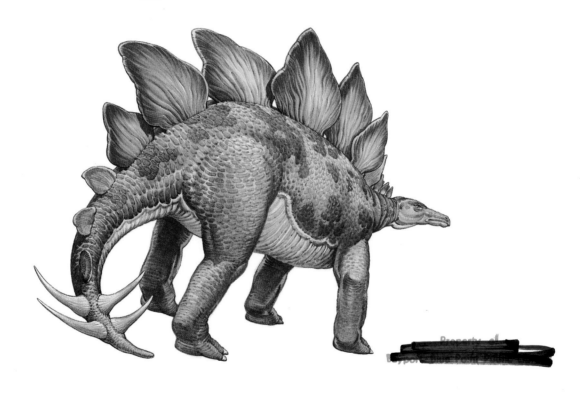

GLENN W. STORRS

Kingfisher
NEW YORK

CONTENTS

INTRODUCTION

Stegosaurus — that dinosaur with the plates on its back and spikes on its tail — is one of those classic dinosaurs of yesteryear. It was originally discovered over a century ago, when the states of Colorado and Wyoming, where it was found, had not had their boundaries drawn, when the Native Americans ruled the Plains, and when dinosaur paleontology was just in its infancy. It was animals like this strange plated and spiked dinosaur that gave people their first glimpse of the richness of dinosaurs in North America.

Over the years, paleontologists have speculated about the lifestyle of *Stegosaurus*. They have focused not only on how the plates and spikes were used, but also why this dinosaur appeared to have such a small brain. Were the plates used for protection against *Allosaurus* and *Ceratosaurus*, meat-eating neighbors of *Stegosaurus*? Were the plates movable? Did they come in a double or a single row? Were they for display? Or did they function as air conditioners and solar panels?

And what of the spikes at the end of the tail? Surely they could have inflicted severe gouges in the legs and even face of a meat eater who came too close! But all of this seems a bit too clever for an animal with very little brain power. For *Stegosaurus* — as well as other kinds of plated and spiked dinosaurs — had very small brains, so small in fact that paleontologists looked elsewhere for centers of stegosaur thought such as between the hips. An intellectual center here seems unlikely, but even so there was space for one! All of these questions and other oddities have surrounded *Stegosaurus* since we began learning about it. The story of *Stegosaurus* and its relatives is a very important one in our understanding of dinosaurs. As part of the early discoveries in North America, *Stegosaurus* gave us our first taste of some of the unusual shapes and sizes of dinosaurs. The life and world of this plated dinosaur continues to fascinate us even today.

David B. Weishampel
Associate Professor
Johns Hopkins University

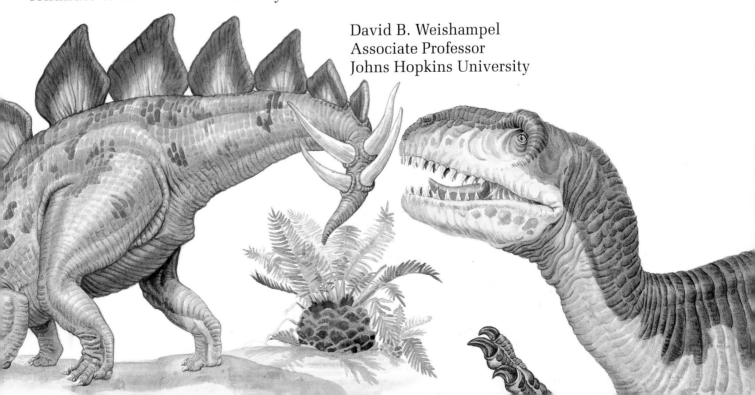

A DINOSAUR TIMELINE

The late Jurassic, about 150 million years ago, is known for its many plant-eating dinosaur species. New types of dinosaurs appeared, among them *Stegosaurus*. Large sauropods like *Apatosaurus* and *Camarasaurus* were dominant, but smaller animals like *Camptosaurus* and *Dryosaurus* were also common. All of these animals were threatened by the hunter *Allosaurus*, which killed and ate other dinosaurs for food. *Stegosaurus* and others evolved bony defenses against *Allosaurus* and its relations. The defenses grew more elaborate, and attackers grew bigger, up until the end of the "Age of Dinosaurs."

Camarasaurus

Ceratosaurus

► The "Age of Reptiles," or Mesozoic era, lasted from approximately 245 million to 65 million years ago. The Jurassic period was the middle portion of the dinosaur "age," coming after the Triassic and before the Cretaceous. The largest known dinosaurs lived during the late Jurassic.

Allosaurus

Stegosaurus

	LATE	TRIASSIC		JURASSIC	
				Early	Middle

Millions of Years Ago

| 230 | 220 | 210 | 200 | 190 | 180 | 170 | 160 |

4

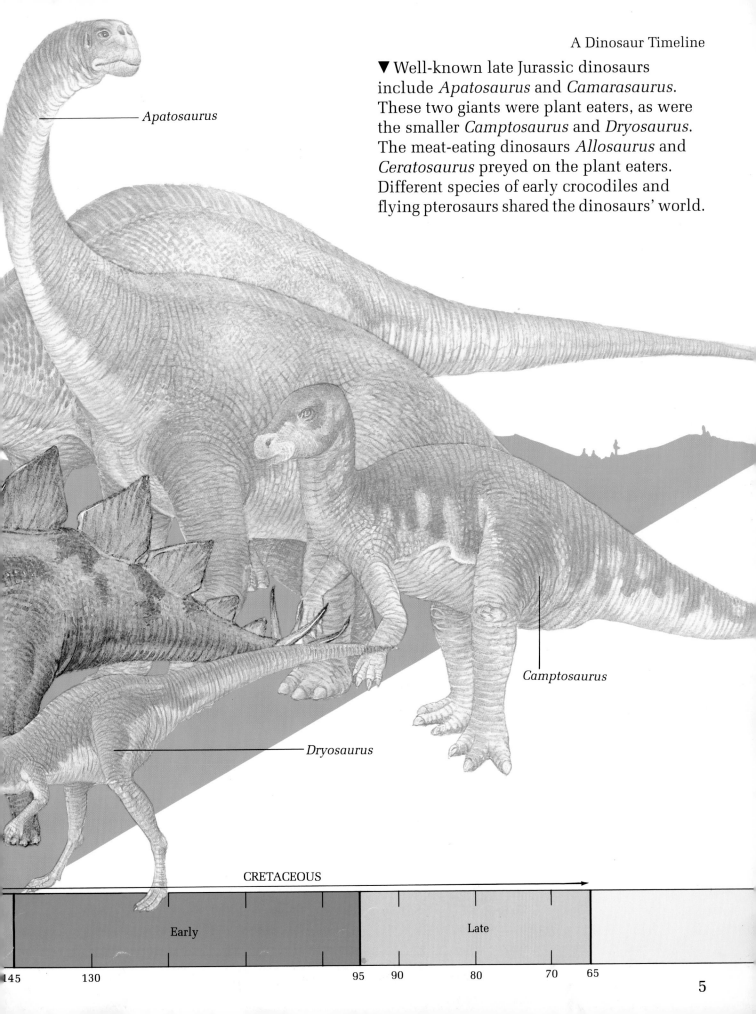

▼ Well-known late Jurassic dinosaurs include *Apatosaurus* and *Camarasaurus*. These two giants were plant eaters, as were the smaller *Camptosaurus* and *Dryosaurus*. The meat-eating dinosaurs *Allosaurus* and *Ceratosaurus* preyed on the plant eaters. Different species of early crocodiles and flying pterosaurs shared the dinosaurs' world.

Apatosaurus

Camptosaurus

Dryosaurus

CRETACEOUS

Early

Late

145   130

95   90   80   70   65

5

150 MILLION YEARS AGO

The Jurassic world was quite different from today's world. The positions of the continents were different and the Atlantic Ocean was just beginning to open. Vast areas of land were low and flat, home to great winding rivers. Lakes and swamps formed from the heavy rains. Mountains were lower than today. North America was partly covered by a warm, shallow sea.

▼ The climate was warmer — monsoonal rain followed long droughts. Lush forests gave plant eaters plenty of food when the rains came. They probably migrated to greener lands in dry times.

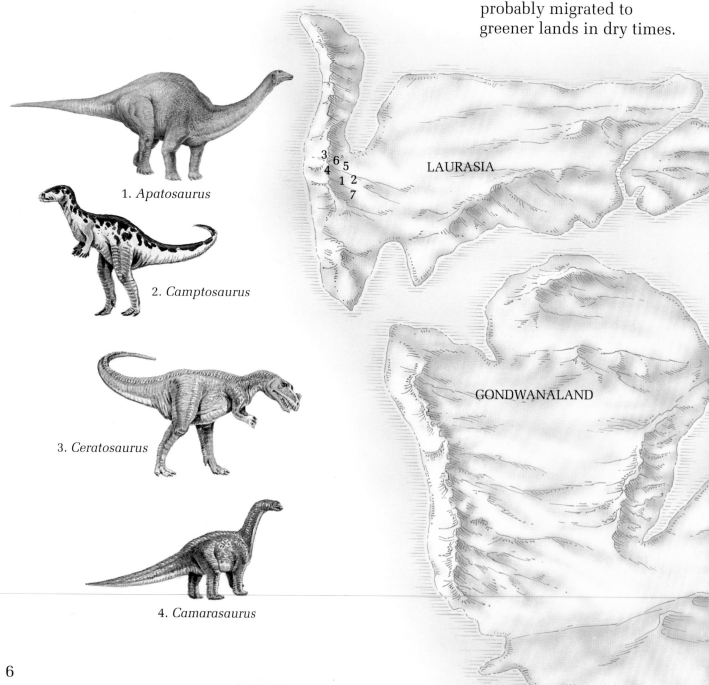

1. *Apatosaurus*

2. *Camptosaurus*

3. *Ceratosaurus*

4. *Camarasaurus*

LAURASIA

GONDWANALAND

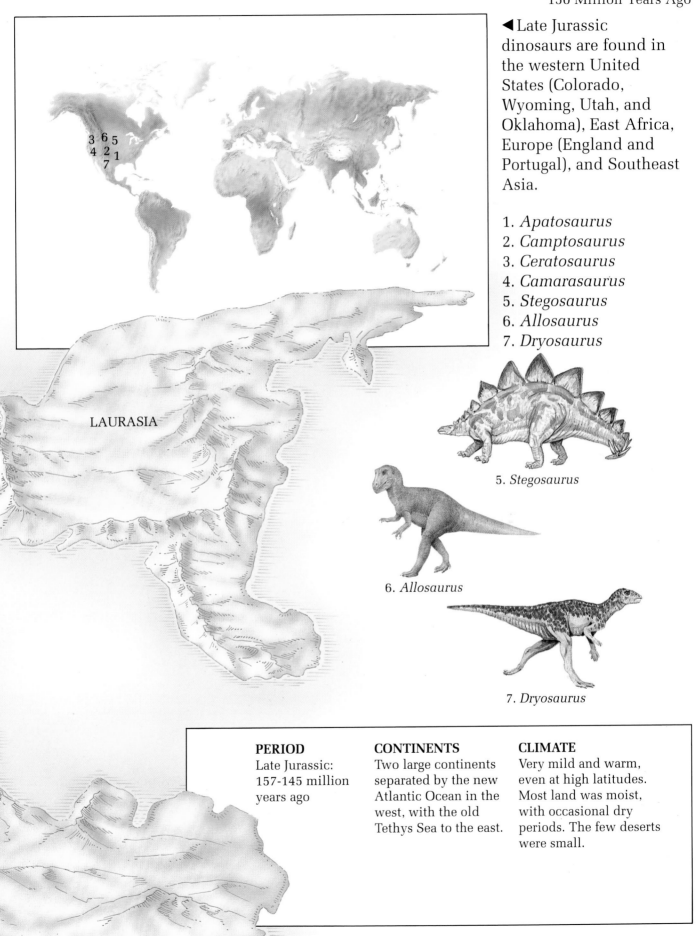

◄ Late Jurassic dinosaurs are found in the western United States (Colorado, Wyoming, Utah, and Oklahoma), East Africa, Europe (England and Portugal), and Southeast Asia.

1. *Apatosaurus*
2. *Camptosaurus*
3. *Ceratosaurus*
4. *Camarasaurus*
5. *Stegosaurus*
6. *Allosaurus*
7. *Dryosaurus*

LAURASIA

5. *Stegosaurus*

6. *Allosaurus*

7. *Dryosaurus*

PERIOD
Late Jurassic: 157-145 million years ago

CONTINENTS
Two large continents separated by the new Atlantic Ocean in the west, with the old Tethys Sea to the east.

CLIMATE
Very mild and warm, even at high latitudes. Most land was moist, with occasional dry periods. The few deserts were small.

JURASSIC PLAIN

Stegosaurus is found in the high plains and Rocky Mountains of North America, in rocks of the Morrison Formation. They were deposited as sediments (sand, mud, and gravel), in huge, slow-moving rivers that once flowed to a warm, shallow sea. The rivers dumped sediments along the way and built great deltas out into the ocean.

▼ Sauropods like *Apatosaurus* walked the flood plains, ate the leaves of tall conifers, and drank from the rivers.

Conifers—

▼ *Stegosaurus* lived along the flood plains. Its bones are found in the muds of the long vanished Morrison rivers.

— Ferns

▲ Birds like *Archaeopteryx* had feathers, but also teeth and a long tail, like their dinosaur ancestors.

◄ *Allosaurus* was a fearsome predator of the late Jurassic. Wherever plant eaters were found, a hungry *Allosaurus* was probably nearby.

Horsetails ——

◄ *Diplosaurus* lived in the rivers and lakes. Modern crocodiles have changed little from this ancient form.

LIFE ON THE FLOOD PLAINS

The muddy flood plains and sandy river banks of the late Jurassic teemed with life. Ferns, cycads, and horsetails growing thickly in the marshy areas made good hiding places for small animals. Moss-covered conifers, ginkgoes, seed ferns, and cycadeoids created thick forests. In places, the river was choked with rotting logs. The hot air was heavy with moisture, and insects were abundant. Primitive dragonflies swarmed in the air, as big and small beetles scurried in the undergrowth or flew from tree to tree.

Plants

Jurassic plants were evergreen — they didn't shed their leaves, for the weather was always warm and heavy rains gave them plenty of water. Plants were evergreen and all green — flowers had not yet evolved.

Fish

Although muddy, the wide river was still home to fish, clams, and snails. Lungfish could gulp air if the water became stagnant.

Ophiopsis

Aspidorhynchus

Turtles

Glyptops hunted small fish, frogs, crayfish, and worms. Turtles also liked to eat soft water plants.

Mammals

Docodon was a small shy mammal, with hair to keep it warm. It probably ate insects, worms, and seeds. It fed mostly at night, when there were fewer enemies about.

Pterosaurs

Flying reptiles called pterosaurs challenged birds in the air. *Comodactylus*, and its cousin *Rhamphorhynchus*, could escape the dangers of the ground by using their wings.

Lizards

Small reptiles scampered through the brush and hid in the trees, chasing insects and basking in the sun.

Insects

Insect life was plentiful. Then, as now, they were more numerous than any other animal group. These are stoneflies.

11

PEACEFUL NEIGHBORS

There were many dinosaurs in the world of *Stegosaurus*. Most were peaceful plant eaters, feeding on the rich foliage of the forest and flood plain. There were no grasses, so they ate low-growing shrubs, or browsed on the leaves and pine-like needles of tall trees. Long-necked sauropods, like *Diplodocus*, *Brachiosaurus*, and *Barosaurus*, could feed on the topmost branches. Smaller dinosaurs, like the ornithopods, preferred easier pickings nearer the ground. All ate huge amounts of vegetation and were constantly alert for signs of their enemies — the meat-eating theropods. Any sign of danger from a nearby predator might cause the plant eaters to stampede.

Camptosaurus

KAMP-toe-SAW-rus
"BENT REPTILE"
23 FT. (7 M) LONG

This common dinosaur walked on broad hooflike toes — either on two legs, or four.

Dryosaurus

DRY-oh-SAW-rus
"OAK REPTILE"
13 FT. (4 M) LONG

The heavy-horned beak of this ornithopod helped it bite through tough leaves and fronds.

Apatosaurus

a-PAT-oh-SAW-rus
"DECEPTIVE REPTILE"
70 FT. (21 M) LONG

Apatosaurus is the best known of the sauropod group of dinosaurs.

FRIGHTFUL FOES

Many animals kill and eat their neighbors for food. There were many large dinosaurs that were enemies of *Stegosaurus.* These meat-eating predators were the theropods. They all walked on two legs, like birds, and had pointed teeth for stabbing and cutting flesh. Paleontologists often find these pointed teeth with the bones of other dinosaurs — proof that they were eaten by theropods. All herbivorous (plant-eating) dinosaurs were at risk from carnivores (meat eaters). Some plant eaters, like the sauropods, traveled in tight herds to protect their young from theropod attack.

Torvosaurus
TOR-voh-SAW-rus
"SAVAGE REPTILE"
33 FT. (10 M) LONG

This rare theropod was as dangerous as *Allosaurus*.

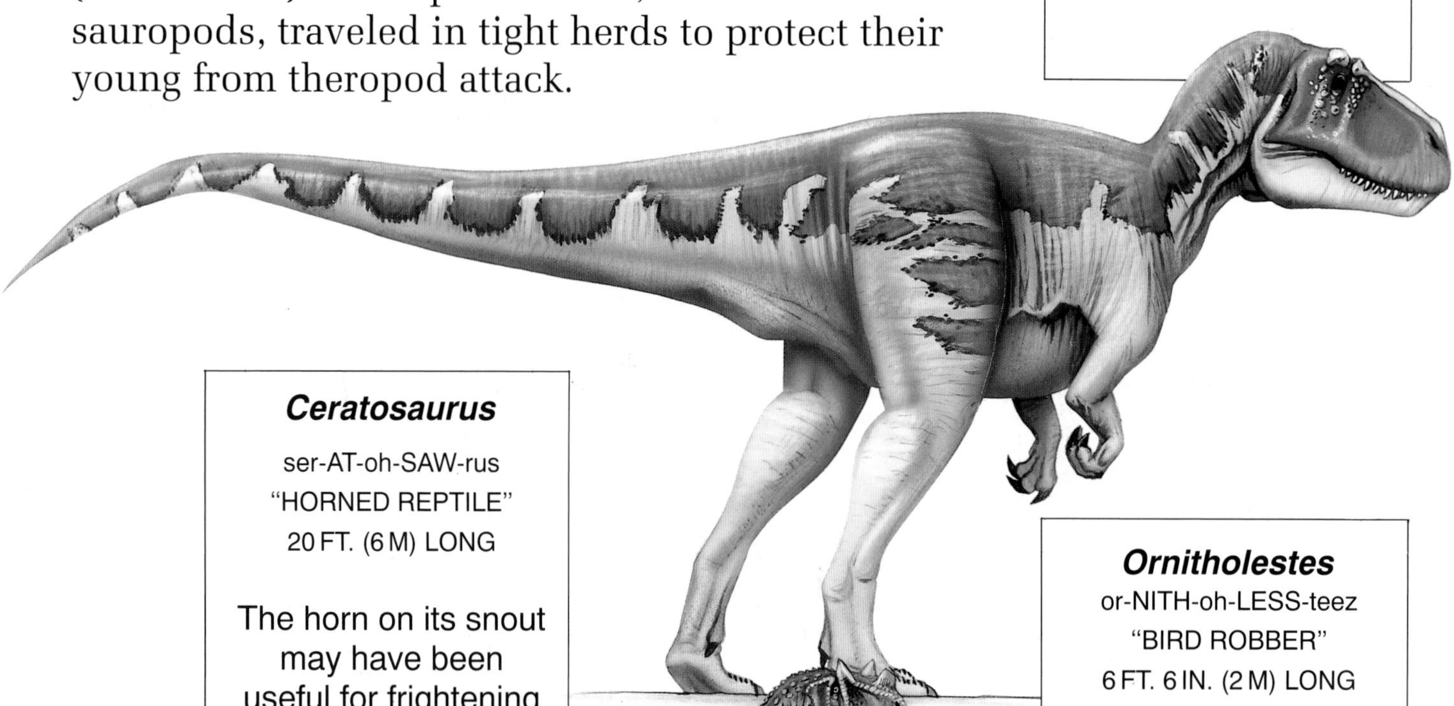

Ceratosaurus
ser-AT-oh-SAW-rus
"HORNED REPTILE"
20 FT. (6 M) LONG

The horn on its snout may have been useful for frightening rivals.

Ornitholestes
or-NITH-oh-LESS-teez
"BIRD ROBBER"
6 FT. 6 IN. (2 M) LONG

This swift runner may have scavenged on dead animals, or stolen eggs and babies.

▼ *Allosaurus* must have been aggressive toward intruders. Threatening glances and a fierce roar might prevent a fight with an outsider.

Allosaurus

AL-oh-SAW-rus

"OTHER REPTILE"

36 FT. (11 M) LONG

The late Jurassic theropod *Allosaurus* was a ferocious hunter and killer. It could easily eat a large plant eater. It tore off big chunks of meat with its sharp teeth and swallowed them whole.

THE ROOFED REPTILE

Stegosaurus is an easily recognized dinosaur, because of its set of back plates. These were large and flat, and projected up from the spine. Its tail spikes are another trademark. Scientists have reconstructed *Stegosaurus*, like most dinosaurs, from single bones and mixed-up skeletons. Paleontology is like a detective story and 3-D jigsaw puzzle rolled into one. It can take years for the bony clues to be dug up, studied, and pieced into a complete animal. It's hard work, but without it, no one would have heard of dinosaurs today. In fact, the word *dinosaur* was first used only 150 years ago. Since then, several hundred species of dinosaur have been discovered.

▶ The paleontologist must imagine the living appearance of a dinosaur. He models its muscles after living animals. Fossil impressions of dinosaur skin show that it was rough and pebbly, almost like an alligator's. The plates of *Stegosaurus* were made thicker by their horny covering.

▶ The bones of *Stegosaurus* show that it had a very small head and a large body. The front legs were much shorter than the back ones, so maybe *Stegosaurus* had an ancestor that walked on its hind legs. *Stegosaurus* had broad feet that gave support to the heavy bulky body. The tail ended in a spray of spikes.

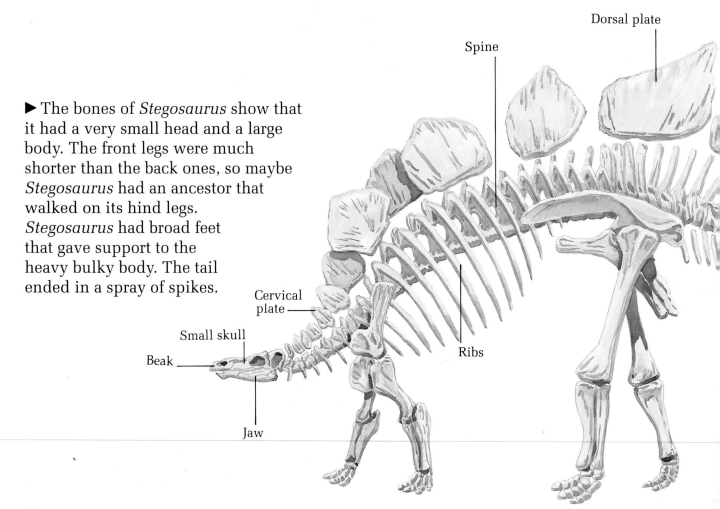

Dorsal plate

Spine

Cervical plate

Small skull

Beak

Jaw

Ribs

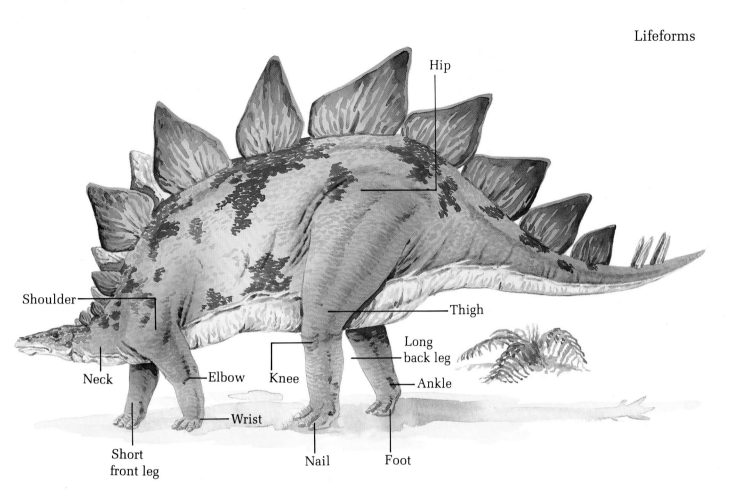

Hip

Shoulder

Thigh

Neck

Long
back leg

Elbow

Knee

Ankle

Wrist

Short
front leg

Nail

Foot

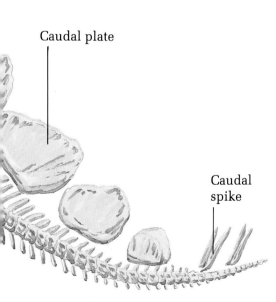

Caudal plate

Caudal
spike

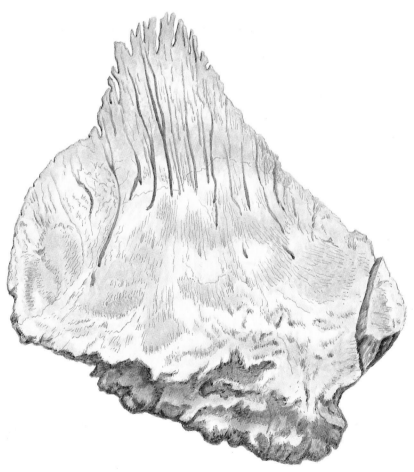

► Each plate of *Stegosaurus* carried
blood vessels. This blood supply
shows that the plate was covered
in living tissue, probably horny
material like a fingernail. The
plate's roughened surface shows
where it was attached.

17

PROBLEMS OF THE PLATES

Stegosaurus plates were unusual things — even for a dinosaur. They were tall and thin, and planted in the skin and muscles of its back, not attached to the backbones. It is therefore hard to know exactly where they belong. Paleontologists have had to use guesswork for the plate positions when reconstructing this dinosaur. Several different ideas about their placement, as well as their use, have been suggested. Even today, not everyone agrees about stegosaur plates and spines. Some scientists believe that the plates were used to control the body temperature of *Stegosaurus*, but we can never be certain. Most scientists think that the plates were a type of armor.

▼ If *Stegosaurus* was too hot, the theory of temperature control says that it moved its plates out of the sun, into the shade or wind.

▲ By basking in the morning sun, a stegosaur might pick up heat with its plates, if the blood in them flowed to a covering of skin.

ELEPHANT EARS

The big ears are not to hear with, but to keep cool in the sun. When they flap in the breeze, the blood in the skin is cooled (like *Stegosaurus* plates?).

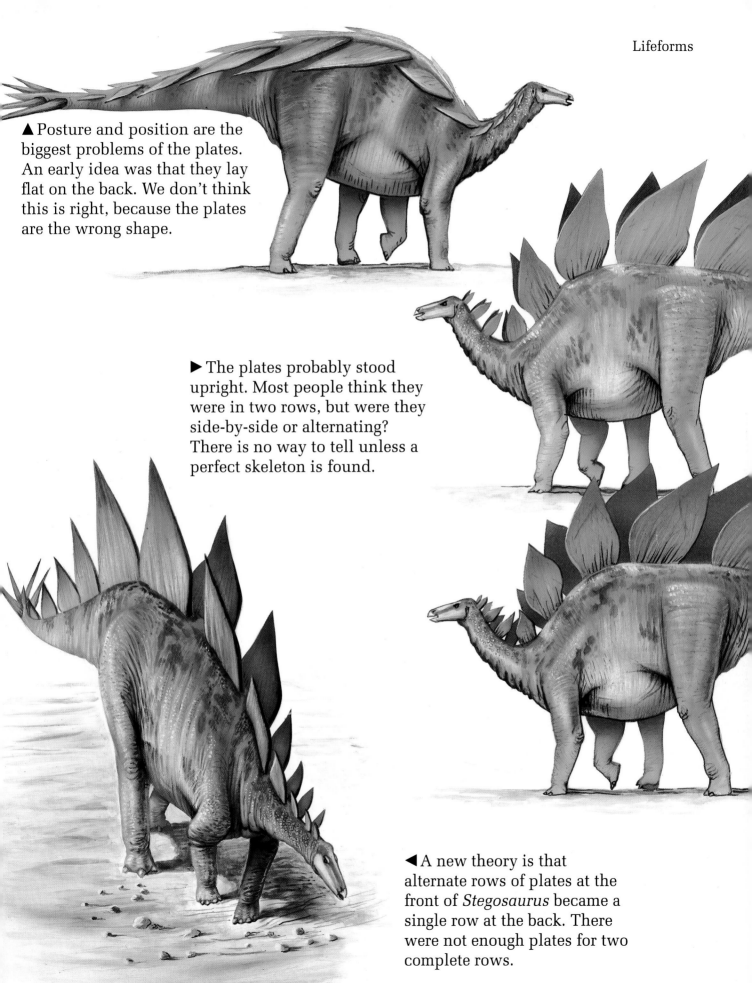

▲ Posture and position are the biggest problems of the plates. An early idea was that they lay flat on the back. We don't think this is right, because the plates are the wrong shape.

► The plates probably stood upright. Most people think they were in two rows, but were they side-by-side or alternating? There is no way to tell unless a perfect skeleton is found.

◄ A new theory is that alternate rows of plates at the front of *Stegosaurus* became a single row at the back. There were not enough plates for two complete rows.

A DEFENSIVE DRAMA

Probably the best explanation for the plates of *Stegosaurus*, is that they were protection from big theropod predators. It would certainly be difficult to bite into a stegosaur's back. The tail, with its four great horny spikes, was probably a "war club" to fend off attackers. Unlike most ornithischian dinosaurs, *Stegosaurus* had no bony rods running along its tail. This means that the tail was especially flexible, and so could be swung against an enemy. A blow from this spiky tail would inflict a horrible wound. A hungry theropod might therefore look elsewhere for its next meal.

▶ *Stegosaurus* must have turned its back and tail toward any advancing threat. Feet firmly planted on the ground, the tail hovered menacingly in the face of danger, *Stegosaurus* would keep a watchful eye on its foe. The horn covering the plates was probably sharp too!

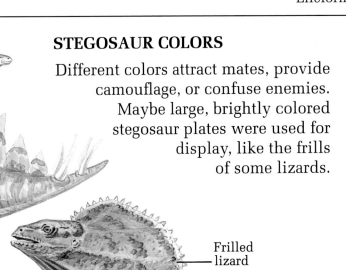

STEGOSAUR COLORS

Different colors attract mates, provide camouflage, or confuse enemies. Maybe large, brightly colored stegosaur plates were used for display, like the frills of some lizards.

Frilled lizard

AGGRESSIVE *ALLOSAURUS*

Predators, such as *Allosaurus*, were wary of the business end of *Stegosaurus*. They had to maneuver around an alert *Stegosaurus*, and try and attack its unprotected sides.

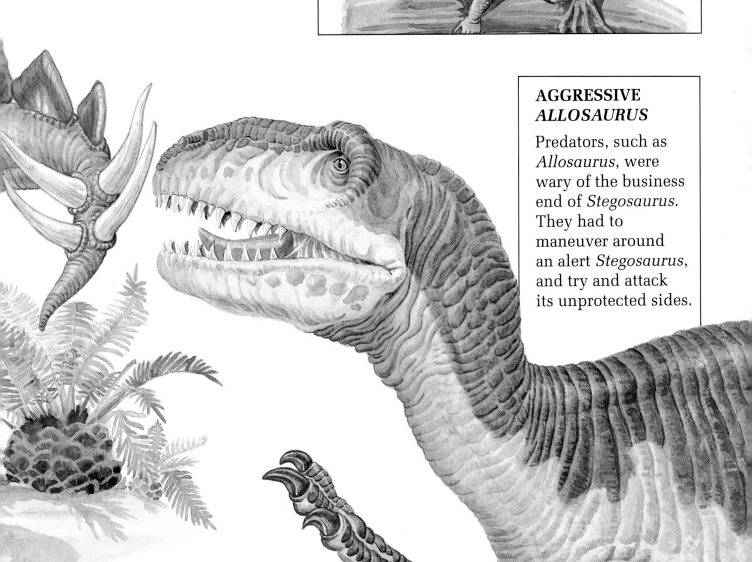

MAKING A LIVING

The bones and teeth of *Stegosaurus* give us many clues about its life. It is the job of the paleontologist to put these clues together. We think that the armor plates and spines were for defense, or perhaps display. What do the other bones of *Stegosaurus* tell us? The teeth show that it was a vegetarian, and since the position of its head was so low to the ground, *Stegosaurus* must have eaten mostly low-growing plants. *Stegosaurus* had to eat and drink, but also give birth to young stegosaurs. Like the babies of other dinosaurs, its young probably hatched out of eggs. Some dinosaurs apparently cared for their little ones; it is likely that *Stegosaurus* brought food to babies too young to leave their nests.

BROWSING

Stegosaurus might have reached fresh, higher leaves by rearing up on its back legs and tail.

YOUNG AND GROWN-UPS

Stegosaurus used its sharp, horny beak to cut up plant food, such as ferns. Its baby did the same soon after birth, for it needed lots of food to grow quickly. It was a miniature version of its mother, but had much smaller plates and spines. These grew larger with age.

▶ Some dinosaurs made nests in the soil, which they covered with rotting vegetation. This kept the eggs warm. *Stegosaurus* laid its eggs in a place safe from danger — away from floods, egg eaters, and the feet of other dinosaurs.

FOOD SUPPLY

Stegosaurus had plenty to eat when the rains came. Did it migrate to greener pastures during the periodic drought?

STEGOSAUR TEETH

Stegosaur teeth were very small and weak. *Stegosaurus, Kentrosaurus,* and *Tuojiangosaurus* could only chew soft plants. Perhaps they swallowed stones to help their stomachs grind up tougher meals.

STEGOSAUR COUSINS

Stegosaurus was only one of many different plated dinosaurs. The Stegosauria flourished in the Jurassic and lived in many parts of the world. The earliest complete stegosaur is *Huayangosaurus* from the middle Jurassic of China, but early stegosaur bones and teeth are also found in Europe. Cretaceous stegosaurs are rare — there are only bits from England, South Africa, and China. The last stegosaur was *Dravidosaurus* from the late Cretaceous of India. Perhaps stegosaurs were made obsolete by their more heavily armored cousins, the ankylosaurs.

▼ *Stegosaurus*, from the late Jurassic of North America, is the best known, and one of the largest, stegosaurs. It also had the biggest plates of any known stegosaur.

Stegosaurus
STEG-oh-SAW-rus
"ROOFED REPTILE"
30 FT. (9 M) LONG

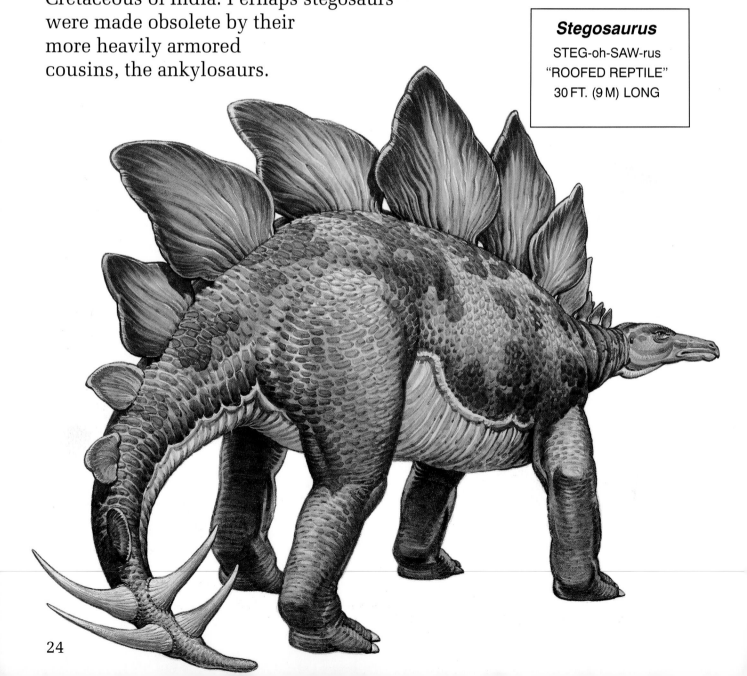

◀ The Thyreophora family tree includes the Stegosauria and Ankylosauria. They evolved from a dinosaur like *Scutellosaurus*.

Scutellosaurus

Scelidosaurus

Scelidosaurus

skel-IDE-oh-SAW-rus

"LIMB REPTILE"

13FT. (4M) LONG

This was a distant cousin of the stegosaurs.

Kentrosaurus

Stegosaurus

Nodosaurus

Kentrosaurus

KEN-tro-SAW-rus

"SPIKY REPTILE"

17 FT. (5 M) LONG

A Jurassic stegosaur from Africa.

Ankylosaurus

Tuojiangosaurus

Toe-JYANG-o-SAW-rus

"TUOJIANG REPTILE"

23 FT. (7 M) LONG

The best known Chinese stegosaur.

DINOSAUR BRAINS

Stegosaurus had a very small brain for its large body — about the size of a doorknob. Obviously, *Stegosaurus* was not very clever, but it was a successful animal, so its brain was big enough for its needs. Even a small brain is a very complex organ. Dinosaur brains can be studied from the petrified sediment fillings of their skulls, or, if the skull is hollow, an artificial rubber mold. The size and shape of the braincase and positions of nerves can be seen in this way. Braincase fossils, called endocasts, show us that most dinosaurs probably acted more like modern reptiles or birds than mammals, relying on keen senses and instinct, instead of intelligence. The *Stegosaurus* brain was one of the first dinosaur brains to be studied. Even today, the study of fossil brains, called paleoneurology, can give us important clues about the behavior of extinct animals.

A SECOND BRAIN?

The hip of *Stegosaurus* had a large space for the spinal cord, giving rise to the myth that it had two brains. In fact, it housed a nerve swelling, called a spinal plexus.

▶ The spinal plexus of the hip cavity was a spot where many nerves met. All vertebrates have a similar nerve swelling. A new theory suggests that the space also held a gland, called a glycogen body, that gave extra energy in times of stress.

◀ *Stegosaurus* was not clever, but it had good movement control. It could probably see and hear well too. Cats have a good sense of smell, as their brain structure shows. The main difference between the two animals, is in the part of the brain used for thinking and remembering.

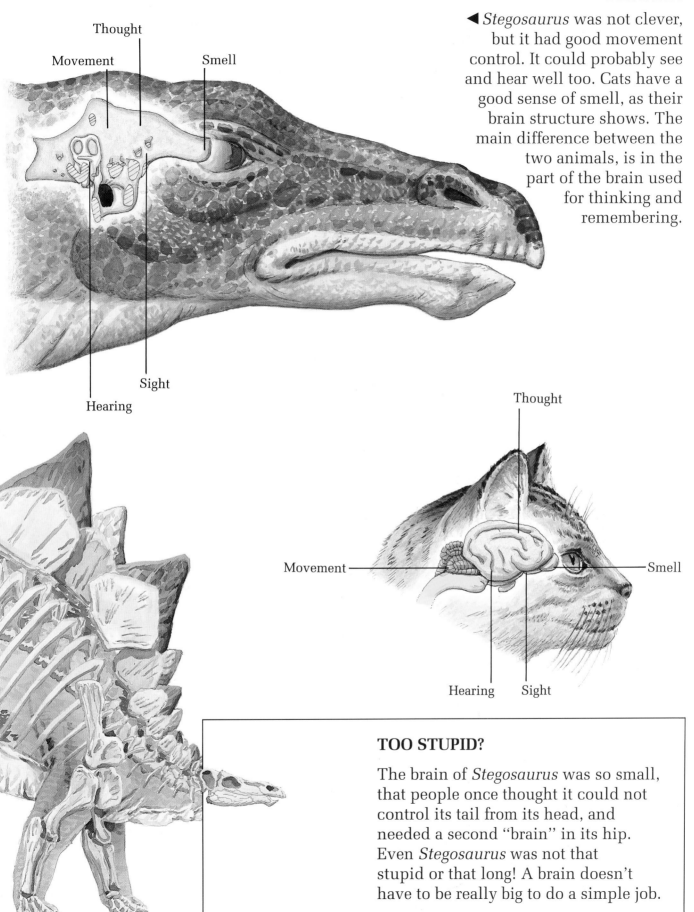

Thought
Movement
Smell
Sight
Hearing

Thought
Movement
Smell
Hearing
Sight

TOO STUPID?

The brain of *Stegosaurus* was so small, that people once thought it could not control its tail from its head, and needed a second "brain" in its hip. Even *Stegosaurus* was not that stupid or that long! A brain doesn't have to be really big to do a simple job.

DINOFACTS

Q: How long did *Stegosaurus* live?

A: Most dinosaurs probably lived to be quite old. Modern turtles may live to over one hundred years, and may grow all during their life. Perhaps very large dinosaurs were just as long-lived. Some dinosaur bones and teeth show growth layers, like the yearly rings in a tree trunk. We might guess how quickly and how long these dinosaurs grew from evidence like this. On the other hand, many dinosaur bones do not have growth rings, but are like those in fast-growing animals. Maybe dinosaurs like *Stegosaurus* grew to a large size quickly, but still lived a long time.

Q: Was *Stegosaurus* slimy?

A: No. Like all reptiles, including snakes, *Stegosaurus* had dry, scaly skin. Because reptiles live mainly on land, they must protect themselves from drying out. The tough scaly skin keeps the body's water in. We also know from the preserved skin impressions of other dinosaurs, that the skin of *Stegosaurus* was probably rough with large, horny scales covering it.

▶ Rare mummified dinosaurs, like this *Edmontosaurus*, preserve the texture of dinosaur skin. The skin was fossilized by hot, dry sand.

Q: How fast was *Stegosaurus*?

A: We don't know, but we can guess. Some dinosaurs have left behind fossil footprints that tell us how they moved. By measuring the distance between the prints, and comparing the length of the leg, we can judge a dinosaur's speed. Sadly, no *Stegosaurus* tracks are known. As the stout limbs of *Stegosaurus* were obviously not built for speed, they probably walked slowly most of the time. *Stegosaurus* did not need to run from its enemies — it was protected by its "war club" tail and defensive plates.

Q: How can you tell the difference between a male and female *Stegosaurus*?

A: The sex of fossils is very difficult, if not impossible, to determine. However, just as in most modern reptiles and birds, a female dinosaur may have been larger than the male of the same species. Maybe a very large *Stegosaurus* was a female. The sexes of some animals are shown in their different colors and shapes. With most deer, a stag has antlers but a doe does not. Perhaps the plates and spikes of *Stegosaurus* were slightly different in males and females.

Red deer

Q: Why did the stegosaurs become extinct?

A: No one knows why they died out. They seem to have been one of the first major groups of dinosaurs to become extinct, and were not part of the "mass extinction" at the end of the Cretaceous age (although the last known stegosaur, *Dravidosaurus*, is from the late Cretaceous of India). Perhaps stegosaurs could not keep up with a changing climate. Maybe, they fell prey to disease, or were out-competed by fitter dinosaurs. If an asteroid killed the dinosaurs at the end of the Cretaceous, this was long after the stegosaurs had gone. Did the giant dinosaurs become extinct through accident, or changing conditions?

Q: Will we ever know more about how *Stegosaurus* lived?

A: We hope so. A new *Stegosaurus* skeleton was recently discovered in Colorado. It may be the best fossil ever found of this dinosaur, and should help to answer some of the questions that still puzzle us about *Stegosaurus*. It is now being studied by scientists at the Denver Museum of Natural History.

► The "mass extinction" at the end of the Cretaceous is one of the great unsolved mysteries of nature.

FINDING *STEGOSAURUS*

Stegosaurus bones are found in the colorful rocks of the Morrison Formation of the western United States. A famous site is at Como Bluff, Wyoming. Tons of dinosaur fossils have been collected here and sent to museums around the world. Professor Othniel C. Marsh of Yale College led teams of students to the American West in the 1870s. His men collected bones of *Stegosaurus*, and other late Jurassic dinosaurs, from a number of dinosaur graveyards, including Como Bluff. Marsh created a sensation by reconstructing the appearance of many of these giant dinosaurs. He also named more new dinosaur species than anyone else.

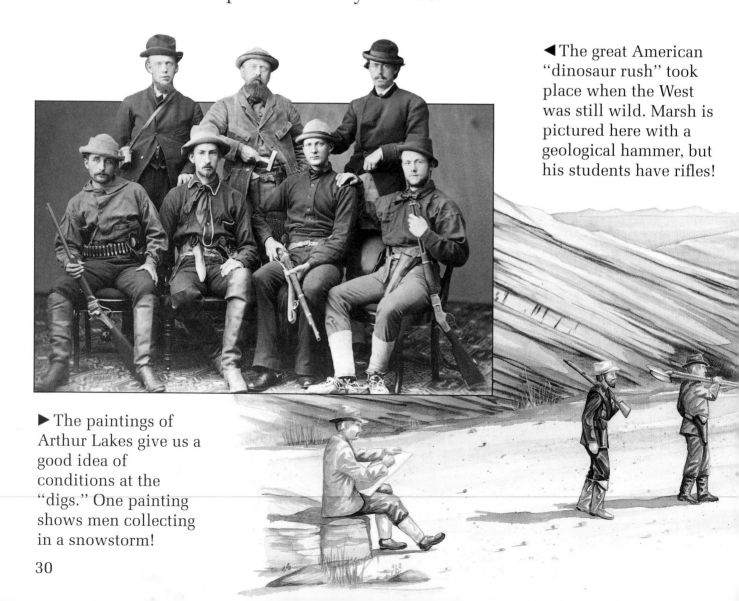

◄ The great American "dinosaur rush" took place when the West was still wild. Marsh is pictured here with a geological hammer, but his students have rifles!

▶ The paintings of Arthur Lakes give us a good idea of conditions at the "digs." One painting shows men collecting in a snowstorm!

30

▶ The first reconstruction of *Stegosaurus* was made by Marsh in 1891. This had one row of plates and too many spikes, but even in the 1890s the basic features were plain.

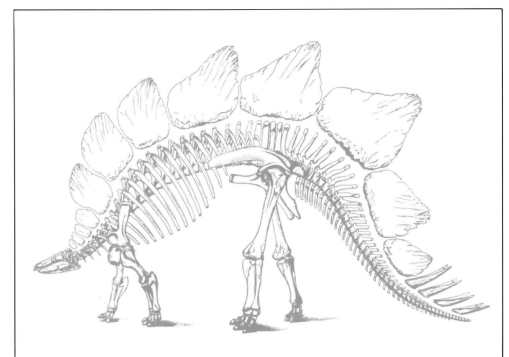

▼ Como Bluff is badland country with gullies and few plants. There is little rain. Paleontologists prefer to look for fossils in places like this, where the rocks are easy to examine and are not hidden by forests or cities! Of course, the rocks must be of the right age.

THE SACRIFICE

All known facts about dinosaurs and their habitats have been entered into a computer program, called DINO, designed by world famous paleontologist Dr. Karl Harlow. He has linked this up to a Virtual Reality machine, with controls that allow the operators to move through the computer-generated landscapes as though they are living dinosaurs themselves. Dr. Harlow has devised a number of "games" that will allow him to observe how dinosaurs may have behaved under certain circumstances. To this, he has added the "Random Effect" — unpredictable consequences caused by the presence of the player in the game.

The players are his children: Buddy, a thirteen-year-old girl, who is brilliant at computer games, and Rob, her ten-year-old brother, who is mad about dinosaurs and wants to be a paleontologist. When "playing" DINO, Buddy and Rob will have to get as close to the "virtual" dinosaurs as possible. They may even have to kill to survive, or become hunted themselves and risk "death by dinosaur!"

"This time it was Rob's turn to strap into the VR machine."

This time it was Rob's turn to strap into the VR machine and enter DINO. His mission was to observe the curious Stegosaurus. It was supposed to have a brain no bigger than a human fist. It was a late Jurassic thickhead, with the body of a truck and the intelligence of a park pigeon. Its other curiosity was the diamond-shaped plates sticking out from its spines. Were they used for armor — that was one theory — or for heat control — like solar panels that could absorb or lose heat, according to the animal's needs?

Rob had to try and interact with Steg and put these theories to the test — theories that his father had some doubts about. Rob made the final adjustments to the VR harness, the finger controls in the glove, and the settings in the VR helmet. He said into his microphone: "All set, Dad."

"OK Rob, you're ready for Mission 2, *Stegosaurus*. Get as close as you can to observe them and remember — look out for that tail! The computer is just selecting your biovehicle." Biovehicle was the name given to the dinosaur that Rob would "become" in DINO. He would have its abilities, its predators and prey. Dr. Harlow was saying, "It's *Dryosaurus*, Rob. Look out for the Random Effect, and if you get in real trouble, exit. This is a game, son, just a game."

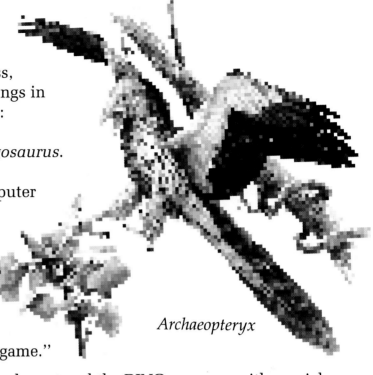

Archaeopteryx

The screen saver of *Pteranodons* dissolved as he entered the DINO program with a quick movement of his hand in the electronically rigged glove. A steamy, swampy scene formed on the stereoscopic screens in his helmet. In the distance, the river shimmered lazily in the midday sun. Hoots, hisses, screeches, and low rumbling noises told Rob that the area was full of late Jurassic lifeforms.

He began his orientation procedure selecting information menus with his "virtual" hand:

"I'm somewhere north of modern-day Colorado, according to the locator. Temperature is upper 80s, humidity high, wind gusty, chance of heavy rain. Terrain is swampy. Selecting DINODATA. I have a group of *Ornitholestes* clustered on the north side of the river, and *Docodon*s among the swamp plants. And I have a small herd of apatosaurs — traveling southward, right toward me like giant bulldozers. Due east, right in the middle of the swamp, are two allosaurs on meat patrol. They could swallow a dryosaur like me whole and spit out the bones. They are also coming this way. No sign of *Stegosaurus*. I'm supposed to work out where he is likely to be — like the Planet of Illusions, eh Dad? Orientation over. I'm beginning to move."

Just as Buddy had done before him, Rob tried out his VR controls and was amazed at how sensitive they were. It really was like being inside a computer game.

Rob began to move north toward the river, away from the patrolling allosaurs, but in the path of the apatosaurs. He knew that unless he stumbled right into their path he would be safe enough. An *Archaeopteryx* glided past him in pursuit of a bright red dragonfly, which it caught and munched loudly in its needle-sharp teeth.

Suddenly, huge teeth-lined jaws exploded from the water and snapped just in front of him. It was a *Diplosaurus*, a prehistoric crocodile, that had been cruising through the swampy waters in search of unwary prey like dryosaurs. Rob moved his middle finger to make a backward step, but *Diplosaurus* came forward again, opening its huge jaws. In these swampy conditions the crocodile creature was too fast. Rob thought quickly, brought up the Random Effect menu on screen, and selected "venom." He then directed with his controls a well-aimed ball of venomous spit at the eyes of the *Diplosaurus*. The blinded animal hissed in agony, writhing its body and thrashing its tail.

Rob didn't wait to see the full effect of this surprise attack. He began to splash through the shallow waters as fast as he could. At one point he fell up to his thighs in the murky gray water and, as he scrambled for a footing, he registered a sharp electronic pain to his lower leg. He moved his head to look down and saw to his horror a water beetle the size of a frisbee attached to his leg. With one swift movement of his scaly front claw, Rob knocked the beetle off his leg. It fell back into the water and sank from sight.

At last, Rob came out of the swamp on to drier land. These attacks had reduced his energy level to 6 and he needed food urgently. He munched on bitter-tasting, low-hanging leaves.

A sound like thunder vibrated in his earphones. But he soon realized that this was no thunderstorm — it was a deep rumbling like bull elephants make, but twenty times louder. Rob then realized that it was the noise made by a creature twenty times the size of an elephant — a creature like *Apatosaurus*!

Apatosaurus

The head appeared first, at the level of the conifers' upper branches. It snatched with its great mouth a vast quantity of leaves, showering the ground with debris. This was accompanied by the sound of crashing undergrowth and splintering branches as it continued on its way. The first

LOCATOR
World

LOCATOR
Local

CLIMATE

GEO

DINODATA

VEG

BIOSTATUS

REPORT

ENERGY

adult was followed by three more adults and two juveniles. Rob assumed they were making the low frequency rumbling noise to communicate with the main herd, a bit like whales do across vast oceans. The land-bound gargantuans left a wake of devastation as they finally passed from Rob's view.

He moved north again, following the curve of the river. As he rounded a bend, he suddenly saw his mission target: two stegs, cropping hungrily at a clump of horsetails. Their movements were slow and deliberate, punctuated with loud grunts and snorts.

"Rob had time to see a group of *Ornithilestes* approach the body of the stegosaur"

DINODATA

ALLOSAURUS

36 ft. (11 m) long. Big head, thick neck, bulky body, and long tail. Serrated, blade-like teeth.

The sky darkened quite suddenly and drops of rain began to fall slowly at first and then cascade as a continuous sheet of water. The stegs disappeared from Rob's screens, and seeing his mission fail before his eyes he decided quickly to cross the river.

"I don't know whether dryos can swim or not, but I don't have time to find a crossing point," he said into the microphone. "This is one way of finding out."

At first, a warning buzzer sounded on the biodata panel, and the OXYGEN DEPLETION light flashed. He moved his limbs with the glove controls in what he thought might be a swimming motion and was surprised when his head broke through the surface of the water. "*Dryosaurus* swims like a fish. It's a great feeling ... oh brother! I've got to get out of this river—and fast!"

Rob had just seen an *Allosaurus* coming through the water toward him. The Virtual heart of the dryosaur and Rob's real heart pounded together as he swam even harder for the bank. The *Allosaurus* was reducing the gap with each second. As it closed in for the kill, it roared its awful sound to disorientate its prey. Rob saw at once that he could not make the bank in time. He quickly calculated the odds and dived before the *Allosaurus* struck. A glancing blow from the huge head sent him spinning under the water. He simultaneously lost vision and balance as he reeled in the VR platform. In the black tumbling waters, he groped for the surface and air. He burst through the surface to find himself right on the pebbly bank, washed downstream from the menace of the allosaur, but also from the stegosaurs, who were now the focus of the *Allosaurus*'s attention. He scrambled up the bank, and peered through the torrential rain in the direction of the stegs. He could just make out the enormous figure of the allosaur emerging from the river, below the bank where the Stegs were still quietly eating, unaware of their danger.

Rob dropped into a gulley and ran along it, now unable to see the stegs. Clawing his way up the side, he reached the top, no more that 150 feet from the stegs, just as the allosaur's head appeared over the bank. The stegosaurs seemed to know it was useless to run. However, as the allosaur approached, roaring triumphantly, the stegs did something quite unexpected. One turned its armored back on the allosaur, and swept its spike-armed tail from side to side like a deadly scythe. It then backed toward the allosaur. It was *attacking*! The allosaur seemed confused. It reared up on its powerful legs and roared even more. Rob had not seen the other steg vanish, but afterward he realized he had witnessed something quite remarkable: one stegosaur had sacrificed itself for another.

It did not take very long for the allosaur to recover. It moved round to lunge at the steg's neck with its daggerlike teeth. Just as the teeth were about to close on to the steg's neck, the spiked tail hit the allosaur below the knee. The allosaur bellowed in pain but did not slow in its attack. Its next strike was better aimed, and the teeth sank into the steg's neck. With a sickening crunch, the teeth severed the spine, and the steg's agonies were over. It fell lifelessly to the ground as the allosaur began its feast. Rob's time in DINO was almost expired, but he had time to see a group of *Ornitholestes* approach the dead stegosaur and steal scraps of meat. He also saw in the distance the other stegosaur, the surviving partner of the allosaur's victim. He thought about trying a ball of spit-venom in the direction of the *Allosaurus*, but those bloodred teeth removed the temptation.

Rob punched EXIT eight seconds before his time expired, and returned with some relief to the real world.

He smiled as he whipped off the VR helmet. Dr. Harlow put an affectionate arm around his shoulder.

"Buddy and I followed your adventure on the monitor. You did well to stay in Rob, that allosaur was out for blood."

"No, I didn't."

"There are very few examples in modern animal behavior where a sacrifice will be made, especially for a partner. Humans are one of the few species to display this. But why not *Stegosaurus*? Without its action of self-sacrifice there may have been two dead Stegs out there. The survivor has a chance at least to continue its genetic line."

"So they might not have been so stupid?"

"Few creatures are stupid Rob, and the *Stegosaurus* proved it was no exception."

"As the allosaur approached, roaring triumphantly, the stegs did something quite unexpected."

GLOSSARY

Ankylosaur ("stiff reptile"): An armored dinosaur with a hard upper shell of bony plates and a club at the end of its tail.

Carnivore ("meat eater"): An animal that eats other animals.

Conifer: A type of evergreen tree, usually with cones and needlelike leaves.

Cretaceous ("of the chalk," after the first limestones associated with the period): The third and last geologic period of the "Age of Dinosaurs" – from about 145 million to 65 million years ago.

Cycad: A tropical, or subtropical, palmlike plant.

Cycadeoid: An extinct plant, resembling a cycad, but only distantly related.

Dinosaur ("terrible reptile"): One of a group of advanced reptiles with an erect posture and straight legs; all now extinct, except for their descendants – birds.

Endocast ("internal cast"): A fossil replica of the inside of the braincase (endocranial case).

Extinction ("wiping out"): The death of a species, or larger group, of animals or plants.

Formation: In geology, a large named unit of rock with some common characteristic.

Ginkgo: A primitive tree with fan-shaped leaves, probably eaten by dinosaurs.

Herbivore ("plant eater"): An animal that only feeds on plants.

Jurassic ("Jura-age," after the Jura Mountains of France, which are made of rocks from this time): The second or middle geologic period of the "Age of Dinosaurs" – from 205 million to 145 million years ago.

Mesozoic ("middle life"): The "Age of Dinosaurs," comprising the Triassic, Jurassic, and Cretaceous periods – from about 245 million to 65 million years ago.

Monsoon: A rainy season controlled by changing winds.

Organism: A living creature, including animals, plants, fungi, and microbes.

Ornithischia ("bird hip"): The group of dinosaurs with a superficially birdlike structure of the hipbones (pelvis). Includes most plant eaters, except for the sauropods and their relations.

Ornithopod ("bird foot"): A plant-eating dinosaur that could stand on two legs and had a stiff tail, such as the duckbills.

Paleoneurology ("ancient nerve study"): The scientific study of the nervous system (brains and nerves) of fossil animals.

Paleontologist ("ancient life studier"): A scientist who studies prehistoric life and its fossil evidence.

Predator: A meat-eating animal that hunts and kills other animals for food.

Pterosaur ("wing reptile"): An extinct flying animal with membraned wings. Not a dinosaur.

Sauropod ("reptile foot"): A giant four-legged, plant-eating dinosaur with a long neck and tail, such as *Apatosaurus* and *Brachiosaurus*.

Sediment: Small bits of rock in the form of gravel, sand, and mud.

Seed fern: A tropical or subtropical fernlike plant bearing seeds.

Species: A group of living things that are similar to each other and can interbreed. The basic unit of classification.

Spinal plexus: A swelling of the spinal cord at the spot near the hip where many lesser nerves meet.

Stegosauria ("roofed reptiles"): The group of plated dinosaurs that includes *Stegosaurus* and its cousins.

Theropod ("beast foot"): A two-legged meat or egg-eating dinosaur.

Thyreophora ("shield bearers"): The dinosaur group that includes the stegosaurs and ankylosaurs.

INDEX

Page numbers in *italic* refer to the illustrations

KINGFISHER
Larousse Kingfisher Chambers Inc.
95 Madison Avenue
New York, New York 10016

First American edition 1994
2 4 6 8 10 9 7 5 3 1 (lib. bdg.)
2 4 6 8 10 9 7 5 3 (pbk.)

Copyright © Larousse plc 1994

All rights reserved under International and Pan-American Copyright Conventions

Library of Congress Cataloging-in-Publication Data
Storrs, Glenn William.
Stegosaurus/by Glenn Storrs.—1st American ed.
p.   cm.—(Dinoworld)
Includes index.
1. Stegosaurus—Juvenile literature.   [1. Stegosaurus.
2. Dinosaurs.]   I. Title   II. Series.
QE862.065S76 1994
567.9'7—dc20   93–43403 CIP AC

ISBN 1-85697-618-1 (lib. bdg.)
ISBN 1-85697-992-X (pbk.)

Series Editor: Michèle Byam
Series Designer: Shaun Barlow
Picture Research: Elaine Willis

Dinoventures are written
by Jim Miles

Additional help from Andy Archer, Cathy Tincknell,
Matthew Gore, Smiljka Surla, and Hilary Bird

The publishers wish to thank the following
artists for contributing to the book:
Adrian Chesterman (The Art Collection), David Cook (Linden Artists),
Eugene Fleury, Terry Gabby (Eva Morris AFA), Adrian Lascom
(Garden Studio), Bernard Long (Temple Rogers), Josephine Martin
(Garden Studio), Roger Payne (Linden Artists), Clive Pritchard
(Wildlife Art Agency), Luis Rey, Guy Smith (Mainline Design),
Studio Galante

The publishers wish to thank the following
for supplying photographs for the book:
The Natural History Museum, London; Yale Peabody
Musem of Natural History

Printed in Hong Kong